W9-BEE-721

Dear Friend:
This ~~book~~ was printed
for us to enjoy — together.
Love,
Betty

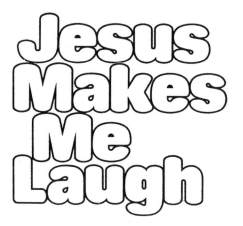

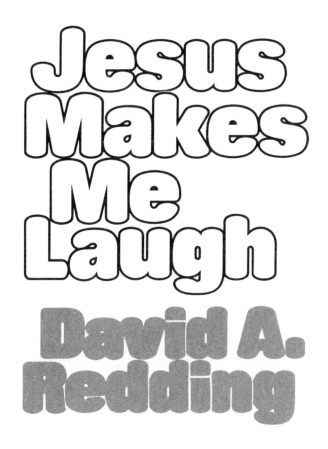

Jesus Makes Me Laugh

David A. Redding

ZONDERVAN
PUBLISHING HOUSE

OF THE ZONDERVAN CORPORATION | GRAND RAPIDS, MICHIGAN 49506

OTHER BOOKS BY THE AUTHOR . . .

The Parables He Told

The Miracles of Christ

If I Could Pray Again

The Prayers I Love

God Is Up to Something

The Couch and the Altar

The Faith of Our Fathers

What Is the Man?

Unless otherwise indicated, Scripture is taken from *The New International Version New Testament,* © 1973 by The New York Bible Society International.

JESUS MAKES ME LAUGH
© 1977 by The Zondervan Corporation
Grand Rapids, Michigan

Library of Congress Cataloging in Publication Data

Redding, David A
    Jesus makes me laugh.

        1.   Christian life—Presbyterian author's.
I.   Title.
BV4501.2.R39   248'.48'51   77 - 10473
ISBN 0 - 310 - 36250 - 04

All rights reserved. No part of this publication may be reproduced, stored in a retrieval system, or transmitted in any form or by any means, electronic, mechanical, photocopy, recording, or otherwise, without the prior permission of the copyright owner.

Printed in the United States of America

To the one who has stayed
devotedly by my side,
my dearest wife, DEE

ACKNOWLEDGMENTS

Velma Young Pierce
Dorothy McCleery Redding
Marion Telford Redding
Doris Woods Cary

CONTENTS

THE JOKE
WAS
ON ME

THE JOKE WAS ON ME

Jesus makes me laugh differently now. I am ashamed to say that in the past I did not laugh with Him, but at His expense. I was not the first. When Jesus told the crowd that the daughter of Jairus was not dead but sleeping, it is said: "But they laughed at him" (Mark 5:40). Let me tell you how my laughter turned from scorn to a redemptive gift.

My father was a pirate — or almost one. He had an offer to play ball with the Pittsburgh Pirates, but he attended a Methodist revival meeting and received the call to preach the gospel. My dad never did anything halfheartedly. He had scrapped his way to the leadership of the gang of boys who worked at the glass house in western Pennsylvania, and he would outswim, outskate, outlift, and outdare anyone, or die trying. That was the way he took on Christianity. He rid himself of everything connected with his old life and became a Methodist circuit rider to twelve churches in the mountains of West Virginia. All he took with him from his old life was his beloved "Flying Simon" gelding, Napper, that he had personally broken and taught to dance and chew tobacco. Dad broke him of both those habits and began working on mountaineers.

My father had only a few weeks of Bible school education added to reading, writing, and frontiersmanship, but he held his listeners fast by his own power of belief in the Christ he found in the Bible and by the big change in his own life.

There were several professional people in one of his churches who were not satisfied by my father's simple Bible messages. They requested a doctrinal sermon. Not to be outdone, dad consulted Thomas DeWitt Talmage, Charles Spurgeon, and Dwight L. Moody and came up with what he was convinced was a masterpiece on "The Proof for the Existence of God." But the King of the Amen Corner, Uncle Henry, was silent that day. After the benediction, my dad characteristically confronted the old man: "Uncle Henry, what did you think of my sermon today?" "Young man, if you must know, I still believe in God despite all you said!" After that dad stuck to the Bible.

However, the days of the circuit rider came to a

close, and my father had difficulty adjusting to a settled pastorate. Also, it was extremely difficult for him to bear the petty grievances and gossip of some small-town church folk. He had been a man's man and had flung everything away for this new life, only to find that many churches were full of hypocrisy, concentrating on the unimportant. He soon had his fill.

One summer he attended a study conference for ministers and encountered higher criticism of the Bible for the first time. It threw him completely. "How could Moses have written the Pentateuch when it speaks of his own death?" "How could Jesus have been poor after the visit of the wise men?" "Why is there almost no evidence outside the Bible for Jesus' life, death, and resurrection?" These questions, added to my father's dissatisfaction with the local church, finished him off. He lost his faith.

Dad left the church and went back to the farm he loved, to raise horses and cattle. I was a teen-ager at the time, I shared my father's love for the farm and his disillusionment with the faith. I was sure of one thing — I would never be a minister.

My mother had been a Scots Presbyterian, and she did not lose her faith and did not give up trying to save me and retrieve dad. But my dad could spot a clergyman a mile off. Working out in the field we would see someone gingerly making his way toward us. "Dave, I'll bet you he's a Presbyterian preacher. I can tell by the way he walks." He was right every time. It was our own private joke.

After three years of active duty in the Navy during

World War II, I entered graduate school in the department of English and was promised a position on the faculty of a college as soon as I completed my doctorate. I particularly enjoyed the subtle ridicule heaped upon the church which seemed to flourish in that department of learning. Any attempt to find meaning in life seemed to me merely a form of madness.

One Christmas, however, when I was still in graduate school, I came home to find that my aunt had sent me another book. She belonged to the Book-of-the-Month Club and, to my discredit, I always surmised that she simply mailed out the books she did not care to keep at the end of the year. This time she had sent *Out of My Life and Thought* by Albert Schweitzer. Whether or not she knew what she was doing, that book was portentous for me. I immediately sat down and read it in amazement.

Perhaps the most learned man of his time, a Ph.D. in philosophy and in theology, one of the world's most distinguished organists and organ builders, Dr. Schweitzer had, in addition to these distinctions, attained a degree in medicine and then left everything and followed Christ to Africa to throw his life away for the natives in pain. It was not an overnight fling. That ministry of healing spanned generations.

Anyone who dismisses Dr. Schweitzer as an unbelieving old liberal simply does not take into account what a vast continent of our faith he recovered by the totality of his sacrifice, and what an impact he made on disillusioned men like me. I am struck to this day by the first words the old heretic always used to say to the patient as

soon as he was regaining consciousness from his opera-
tion: "The reason you have no more pain is because the
Lord Jesus told the doctor and his wife to come to the
banks of the Ogooue."

I shared with my father that book and the effect it had
on me. I also told him that I had decided during that
Christmas vacation not to return to my English studies, but
to transfer to a graduate school of divinity. "Dad, I don't
know what I think about God, but I want to find out." He
replied: "Dave, if you have to go, find the most liberal
school there is; look in every corner and under every
stone for the answer to every question so you won't have
the rug pulled from under you halfway through your life
as I did."

I found a divinity school so liberal that we didn't
come to the Bible until about two weeks before com-
mencement. We were taught to smile with a certain
indulgent condescension when anyone mentioned Billy
Graham's name. The ridicule of anyone enthusiastic
about Christ was relaxed and subtle, so all the more
cutting. If anyone were to sob out loud how Christ had
saved him from the jaws of hell, we were by implication
cleverly taught to respond: "That's very interesting."

A man could cut his heart open for us to see his Christ
and collapse in his seat in tears, and we would still say:
"That's very interesting." You would have thought we
might have exclaimed: "My God, where do *I* find such a
Savior?" But no, even now in the proper theological
schools it is considered bad form to blurt out the "good
news" so personally.

About this time I became engaged to a girl who was

taking a degree in Christian Education at a conservative seminary and who devoutly believed in the things that I was disregarding. We began to argue about religion, and for some reason we used up reams of paper in correspondence on the subject of hell. I could not believe in hell. She could not believe that I didn't. Finally she went to her favorite professor to see if he would advise breaking off the engagement in view of such heresy as mine.

He counseled her to remain engaged. "It will take care of itself." He was right. After a few years of married life, I was finally able to grasp the difficult theological concept of hell! (I usually say this in my wife's forbearing presence, for it is really through her that I have learned of heaven.)

However, even during my first years in the ministry, what I knew about God kept me from God. From one point of view seminary is indispensable, but from another it simply multiplies the avenues of escape. I preached on ethics and on controversial issues. Where was the strength? I treated Christianity as something to chew like gum. What about bread? It was safer to talk God over instead of letting Him take me over. My trips to the grave and to the hospital were pitiful and sterile. Someone had stolen my thunder.

One night about two o'clock the phone rang. It was a young nurse calling from the hospital. She was crying. "Mr. Redding, do you remember little Jamie with leukemia?" "Yes." "He just died, and his parents are here calling for you. Could you come now?" I think something got through to me then — that they should think that I would have something necessary to say to them. Surely there was something that needed to be said or done for them. But it was beyond me.

About that time I felt I should try preaching on miracles instead of parables. After all, the miracles take up a vast part of the gospels. I had avoided the miracles, and I found I had trouble getting into them because I did not consider them to be historical events. I had been a devotee of Rudolph Bultmann who held that Christ's miracles were helpful myths. The tragic result of this "sophisticated" position is that it really cancels out the impact of the miracles. Why bother with them if they didn't happen? Bultmann and his followers hold that these stories yield insights, but to be told the miracles did not actually occur in effect removes them from serious consideration or from conveying any claim of Christ over a man's life. Bultmann's view is a kill-joy. Who will respect sermons on such uneventful subjects which the apostles had made up only to promote Christ? Why should I pick my dreary way through the wreckage of our faith like a souvenir hunter, searching for something I would have to substantiate with modern psychology?

I wondered if there were a scholar I could trust who actually believed in the miracles of Christ as historical events. While I had been taught to distrust the scholarship of those who did believe in them, C. S. Lewis helped me by destroying my confidence in Bultmann's concept. Lewis held the distinguished chair of Medieval and Renaissance Literature at Cambridge University in England and was probably one of the world's foremost authorities on the genre of myth. Lewis insisted that the miracles of Christ had none of the characteristics of myth. He did not feel that his intellectual integrity had been compromised in the least by his becoming a Christian who believed the gospel as the Word of God and the miracles as the acts of His Son our Lord on earth.

Nonetheless, I kept looking for a scholar I could trust who believed that the miracles were historical. Once again the Book-of-the-Month Club came to my rescue. They were offering a copy of the sixty-dollar Rembrandt Bible free to new members. Rembrandt was no fool, and yet he was still preaching through his paintings to so diverse an audience as the Book-of-the-Month Club. I joined, and as soon as I received my copy, turned to see what Rembrandt did with the most difficult miracle of all — the raising of Lazarus from the dead.

Rembrandt had a powerful painting on this subject, and it was quite obvious that Lazarus was not being raised in spirit only. The reanimated and bandaged corpse was realistically coming to life. Then I happened to turn to the back of the painting to see what the critic said of it. Critics have done so much harm, but the words that critic left there helped me into the Lord's bright blessing: "Rembrandt did everything he could think of to intensify the effect of the miracles of Christ." I had intended to dampen their effect, but Rembrandt did everything he could think of to enhance them, to give them glory. For some reason those words of that unknown critic did me in. From then on, I too tried to do everything I could think of to intensify the effect of the miracles. When I turned that page, I changed sides.

I decided to preach on the raising of Lazarus from the dead at the Easter service, although I had never before heard a sermon on it. I was completely fascinated by that story. The reader is immediately aware that it is stranger than fiction. It is the kind of self-evident event that could not have been fabricated. It had to have happened.

Lazarus, Jesus' friend, becomes ill. His sisters, Mary and Martha, send for the doctor, Jesus, but He refuses to come until Lazarus is good and dead. When Jesus finally arrives, Lazarus has been dead four days. The sisters scold Jesus for His bewildering delay; then they are as appalled as any Ivy League professors could be to discover that Jesus has not returned to pay His respects, but to bring Lazarus back to life.

Bitter disappointment in the sisters now gives way to utter horror as they realize that Jesus is about to make a fool of Himself and be an embarrassment to them all forever. Martha uses the strongest language she can think of to stop Jesus: "Lord, he stinketh." Jesus is immovable. At the graveyard He thanks God for raising Lazarus even before looking to see if His praying is effecting any vital signs. His bridges are burned. Then in a loud voice Jesus shouts: "Lazarus, come forth!"

I had never raised my voice in that Presbyterian pulpit before, but that day, since John had said that Jesus shouted, I shouted those words as loudly as I could. And for the first time in my life someone asked me for a copy of my sermon.

Our intellectual understanding is not the reason we disbelieve in God, the gospels, or the miracles. Nor is it because we are too smart for them or because we have outgrown them. No. As a distinguished nuclear physicist reminded me recently, the block to our belief is our will.

Our minds are the nimble tools of our wills, and they quickly formulate the mental position that pleases us — that suits our wishes. It is the will of man that must be broken, not the mind, for conversion affects our ego. Our mind is only the willing slave of what we want. The reason behind my slow surrender to God was really that I preferred to be God, or to be free of the demands such a belief would surely make of me. Aldous Huxley confessed before he died that the reckless moral and religious position he had taken was simply to suit himself, not because of careful research.

I reported to my dad that so far as I could, I had looked into every corner and turned over every stone in my effort to school myself — and for his sake too. I had finally come to the conclusion that long ago when he began preaching to the people what the Bible said, through the uncluttered eyes of his great love for Christ, he had not been far from the kingdom. Whether dad needed the confirmation of my search or whether God gave him grace in other ways, he did die believing and able to say once more the lines he loved: "By faith Abraham, when called to go to a place he would later receive as his possession, obeyed and went, even though he did not know where he was going" (Heb. 11:8). I had it engraved on the stone where his body lies, for him and for me.

It seemed my father was calling to me, like an aging and imprisoned John the Baptist, to go ask Christ for him: "Are you the one who was to come, or should we expect someone else?" And the answer came back from the only One who could answer it, graciously, powerfully, and with such love: "Go back and report to John what you hear and see: The blind receive sight, the lame walk, those who have leprosy are cured, the deaf hear, the dead are raised, and the good news is preached to the poor. Blessed is the man who does not fall away on account of me" (Matt. 11:3-6).

BOOGER AND SMILEY

BOOGER AND SMILEY

Booger and Smiley were two of the best surfers on Florida's east coast and two of the worst for "raising hell," but God used them to continue my lesson in laughter. Smiley had once distinguished himself as the best spitball shooter in our Sunday school, but other than that this pair had laughed God off.

As in most communities across our country, some of the churches in St. Augustine clung to a fistful of youth who came either to church school or a youth group. Most came out of a sense of duty or because they had nothing else to do. Some youth were forced to attend as a punishment because they had received poor grades or been late getting home at night. The typical church youth group is regarded as a drag, out of touch with God and young people. This is why most young people don't come and why it wouldn't make much difference if they did.

I have visited numerous youth groups in churches across the country. The atmosphere is lethargic and reproachful. The discussions seldom reach the gut level. Those present grill each other about their sloppy attendance. "How are we ever going to get more kids out if our own officers don't show up?" The sponsors are always resigning. Every now and then someone suggests, "Let's have a series on different religions, or on drugs, or on sex," but so far as relating where the youth are to where Christ is — nothing doing.

Christ is not alive at such meetings. He is carried in feet first. He is not really invited to come in on His own and take over. Jesus is a dogma spread over the proceedings. This is the way the church dies — manipulating the arms and legs of Christ in a macabre dance of death. They have discussions, not confessions. They have Bible games, not live contact. This kind of demoralization has gone on for so long now no one thinks anything of it. Church members keep thinking that all the youth group needs is one more go-getter minister or another change in sponsors. It doesn't occur to anyone that there is a more excellent way.

Like many ministers, I did not need much encouragement to think that I understood young people. Who will reach the next generation if we experts who have slaved in the seminaries don't do it? I am ashamed to say how many years it has taken me to learn that my knowledge about God has gotten in God's way. For as soon as I acknowledged that God was not reaching the high school through me, as soon as I got out of God's way, God swiftly sent us an attractive college junior through the Young Life organization to start a club in our town.

Bill was handsome but real. He had gotten religion the hard way. He and a girl named Sally started with a guitar and six kids in our living room. Our family made two indispensable contributions: We supported the cause and kept out of the way. These are the two most difficult challenges for a minister!

One Wednesday night Bill promised that he would swallow a goldfish when the group of six grew to one hundred. A few months later he swallowed it. But Bill and Sally did not give away their secret on Wednesday only. They hung around the high school along with the drug pushers. What they did was not so much "witness" as "withness." They went where the kids were and loved them the way they were. They didn't start with the church kids, but with the leaders in the high school hierarchy. "How about coming to the club Wednesday night?" "What goes on?" "Come and see."

Kids came in droves. That fall one hundred and fifty met weekly in Catholic and Protestant living rooms. Teen-agers do not know a denominational Christ. At our house they shoved our "Early Salvation Army" furniture up against the wall and everybody jammed together on the floor. This was part of the magic. Have you ever heard the typical youth group raise the roof? This gang sang so loud that the neighbors complained. They sang to God:

"Oh, they whipped Him up the hill . . . they pierced Him in the side . . . and He hung His head and died . . . for me." One skeptical Episcopalian parent told me in tears how God got to him as he overheard them singing that song.

Police checked on the club one night because one member of the force had grown suspicious. "There aren't that many cars parked out there for nothing." That incident increased attendance. When we had asked the high school principal's permission for Bill and Sally to hang around the school building, we asked him not to give the club his public approval. To kids that is the kiss of death. All we needed from him was approval behind the scenes. Adults were not to recommend this club to kids. Teenagers found it for themselves. This was their God, not their parents' God. Club Night became the big night of the week. Doesn't that remind you of: "I came that they might have life, and far more life than before"? I knew something had happened when I discovered that parents were punishing their kids by preventing them from coming.

Booger and Smiley decided to go to club one night. They laughed at the skits and intended to keep on laughing. Then Bill stood up holding his *Good News for Modern Man.* He opened it to the ninth chapter of John and started talking about this really neat guy towering over a boy born blind. Bill imitated the darting vacant eye movements of the blind. "The big guy asks the boy, 'Do you want to see?' Astounding question! His voice doesn't sound as though He's kidding. The blind youth is flabbergasted by such a proposition, but thinking this may be his big chance, he stammers out, 'Uh, yeah.' Then he hears the big guy spit and hears Him making two mud balls. These He plants into the unseeing eyes. Then the blind boy gets his directions. 'Go wash in the pool.' And somehow, instead of getting exasperated with these antics, the blind fellow sprints for Siloam pool holding on to his mud packs. 'God in heaven, he sees!' ''

But Bill didn't leave the matter back there in Palestine. ''Some of you guys here tonight can't see too well either.'' There is a hush. ''Do you want to see?''

Of all the people in the world, Booger and Smiley wanted to see. And as surely as the blind man could see back then, they began to see too. I don't mean it was only an emotional spree. They kept coming back week after week. ''You shall know them by their fruits.'' Even the girls down on the beach kept asking, ''What's gotten into Booger and Smiley? You wouldn't believe how different they are.'' I too wanted to test the authenticity of such a change. That next fall I told Booger and Smiley that I realized something seemed to be happening to the senior highs in town, but ''now the junior highs are going to hell. Do you care?''

Booger and Smiley showed up at our little denominational junior high group, and by the next week they were leading it. The attendance jumped toward a hundred, including many youngsters who were not from our church. There was guitar music and singing, skits heavily sprayed with shaving cream and water, and a brief personal message from Booger or Smiley. And following Bill's example of close relationship with them, both hung around the junior high school and the boat ramp.

They planned and held a retreat at which one hundred and seventeen junior highs paid eight dollars apiece to attend. Frightened mothers phoned when they learned who the leaders were, but no one canceled out. Perhaps that was a sign of how desperate parents had become. We rented buses, stood by and paid bills, but tried to keep out of the way. Things happened out there. I asked fourteen-year-old Paul to tell us what happened to him. He looked down at his feet and declared, "God has been knocking on my door for a long time, but I've always kept the safety chain on. Last weekend I took it off." More retreats followed. Booger and Smiley had something that bore fruit.

I decided it was time for them to share this in the church service itself. I asked Booger to offer the invocation and Smiley the pastoral prayer in morning worship. This may not seem very radical, but our church was extremely sedate and formal. In the sanctuary one looked up almost one hundred and fifty feet into the dome. It was no place for children playing. Or was it? What worried me most was not the departure from our customary use of older people, but the reaction to the boys' long hair. This was before most of us had had a chance to adjust to that style.

I foresaw one other problem. One must never tease a Presbyterian minister about his pet, the Sunday bulletin. He delights to see it letter-perfect, so it is proofread repeatedly. Abbreviations or vulgarities are scrupulously eliminated, and all Christian and middle names and titles are spelled out. I loved that bulletin, and during my spare time loved to read old issues. But as the printing deadline approached for our Sunday with Booger and Smiley, I ingratiatingly informed them that naturally we would have to use their Christian names in the official church bulletin. To my dismay they, who had been so Christian in all other respects, dragged their feet on this. "Oh, no, Rev, nobody would know who we were." So that morning beside the Prelude the bulletin read: Johann Sebastian Bach; and beneath that, Invocation: Booger.

As Booger and Smiley processed into church with me that morning, I saw the stares and looked in vain for an exit in the chancel area. I had warned my young assistants to write out their prayers ahead of time, since God doesn't always put words into one's mouth in public. I thought Smiley had appreciated that, for he was carrying a yellow tablet. But while I gave the Call to Worship, I heard Smiley whisper behind me: "Booger, where's your prayer?" "I don't have one." "What are you going to do?" "I just now thought of one."

Then Booger, with his blond hair waving, stood to pray in a surprisingly loud voice: "O God, bless all the men here with long hair, and all those with short hair, and all those with no hair, and help them to love each other for Christ's sake. Amen."

This reminded me that "Your sons and daughters will prophesy, your young men will see visions" (Acts 2:17). But you are wondering, as I did, how the older people reacted to Booger's prayer. Several weeks later my wife asked the women in her circle if they would share the last time they actually experienced communion. One distinguished grandmother declared: "The day those boys prayed for us in church." The editor of the newspaper wired the prayer over the national news service.

All of this spiritual excitement among the youth profoundly affected the church life in town. You can't have anyone running into Christ without its spilling over into other lives. The front center section of our church had been empty for years; now it was regularly filled by young people.

Smiley felt the call to go into the ministry. He is now in his middle year in seminary, and while in college he assisted in our regular worship service. Booger gave his major paper on Jesus in the college religion class I taught and received the only applause I ever heard them give. He and Smiley inaugurated a college Bible study, and Booger's older brother, Joe, a favorite of mine, succeeded Bill as our Young Life club leader.

The effect of Young Life was evident in the emerging and forthright sharing of several small groups. Our Sunday morning group met in the church gardens between services one Easter. You will recall that a garden is where it happened. It is happening still. About forty of us were sitting in a circle. Instead of the old-style lecturing, it was an experience in sharing, and the effect was not so much informative as it was recuperative. We learned much of this from the local Young Life's "Broken Drum" program. The aim was not to teach each other something so much as to bless and relieve each other and rediscover what we already knew in our hearts. Our question that Easter morning was: "What would you like God to do for you next?" We went around the circle for the answers: "I need patience." "Tell me how to love." "To know how to tell others what is happening to us."

How deeply moved we were! After everyone had

had his say, the opportunity was given for each person to pray a sentence prayer for someone in the group whose need had touched his heart. Several prayed out loud for the first time. A twelve-year-old Puerto Rican girl and her little brother had slipped into the group that morning, and each of them prayed. There were no dry eyes in our church group that Easter. It is a wonderful thing to hear prayers so serious that they are for specifics; but to pray for a specific person is one of the most beautiful experiences I know. Christ will come every time.

Booger and Smiley profoundly affected our church as well as the Christian life in our community. It was the same gospel, unafraid to be contemporary, spontaneous, and individual. And as with our Easter group, the leader spoke less and everybody else more. Our church became more welcoming, more tolerant of dress and appearance. Sympathy and understanding were awakened to "even these least ones" as well as to the stranger and the strange.

The church's cross-fertilization also blessed Young Lifers. After all, Christianity is not a sect with hair restrictions in either extreme, and the guitar is no more or less sacred than the organ. If the church is really the church, it has room for old Franciscans, black Quakers, Jesus freaks, Catholic Pentecostals, and Chinese Dutch Reformed junior highs.

Since we have paid tribute to Booger's invocation, I ought also to confess the benediction that Jabo Cox gave in our church. We had invited Young Life to hold its southeast district meeting in our town. Church people were invited to attend the meetings, and one of the highlights Saturday night was the music of Jabo Cox, director of Young Life's urban work in Florida. So I asked Jabo if he would give the benediction with his guitar in the worship service the next morning. What Jabo did with that benediction perhaps best illustrates the effect of Young Life on that town.

Jabo had been a heroin addict for eight years. It showed in his face, though he was still a young man. Something changed Jabo until now he worked magic on other kids with a guitar in the ghetto which had been his home for years. The last hymn had just been sung in our formal Presbyterian church. Everyone was standing. The man with the weathered face walked to the front of the church, just as an impressive-looking latecomer entered the east doors.

Jabo played two brief songs. The first was his story, how he dropped out of school at thirteen and went from "grass" to hard drugs. He sold his body to men to pay for his addiction. It was dark where he was, dark as death. It was hell.

Then something happened. Morning came. "My life came back to me. It made it possible for me to graduate from high school at thirty-eight. The best way to tell you what happened is by my last song." The lean face of the man who had seen hard times beamed. The standing worshipers were hushed. "You all know this song," he said. "Won't you sing it with me? It's my favorite."

Then Jabo began to sing: "Jesus loves me, this I know, for the Bible tells me so." I don't know when that song had last been sung in that church. It was sung in Sunday school. The people were so moved they couldn't sing. Jabo stopped and looked around the beautiful sanctuary. His face reflected what he had been through. "It seems to me," he said, "that Jesus has been mighty good to you folks. Won't you sing the rest of it with me? 'Little ones to Him belong. They are weak, but He is strong.' " Only a few sang with him — not because they wouldn't, but because they couldn't.

When I walked out, I went to the doors where I had seen the latecomer enter. He was still standing back there. He wrenched my hand and introduced himself as an executive of a large firm. His eyes were tearful and red. "Pastor, I'm sorry I was so late I missed your sermon, but I arrived in time for the benediction, and that was all I needed."

How beautifully God picks up the pieces to put His message together. We all know how hopeless ignorant fishermen and heroin addicts are, but Jabo has been working for years now in the inner city putting heart into "cast-off" kids.

"Jesus Loves Me" is for babies, isn't it? And yet Karl Barth, one of the greatest theologians of modern times, when asked to put the Bible into a sentence, quoted this song. Name the last person you met who was saved during the benediction. I dare you to let Booger or Jabo do the sermon. I tremble at what was accomplished by letting them have a little opening and closing prayer.

It has been fashionable for some time now for ministers and churches to conform to the world's scorn of Christianity's most precious beliefs. The church is a mission field. I am ashamed to confess that it may be its own worst enemy. Malcolm Muggeridge, former editor of *Punch* magazine and one of Britain's prestigious literary and television figures, has become a Christian. He has this to say about clergy:

> We have grown used to clergymen adopting all sorts of positions, from glorifying *Playboy* Magazine to detecting spiritual undertones in cults like Mau Mau. . . . Many clergymen are particularly drawn to any movement or position which denigrates the Christian religion and its Founder. Having, perhaps, lost their faith, but being committed for one reason or another to their cloth, they derive great, if unconscious satisfaction from anything that undermines the one and discredits the other.[1]

Perhaps it is now the church that is white unto harvest, and God is scraping up some outside messengers such as Booger and Smiley to send in from the fields. Isn't that a laugh? Yes, in the most beautiful way.

[1]Malcolm Muggeridge, *Chronicles of Wasted Time* (New York: William Morrow and Co., Inc., 1973), p. 55.

THE LORD OF THE DANCE

THE LORD OF THE DANCE

There were sixty of us. We had a week to spend in a canyon one hundred and twenty miles northwest of San Antonio. We stayed in elegant suites of stone and glass worked into the bluffs above the spring-fed river. In the clear water below us huge catfish waited for us to bait them. Across the canyon on the opposite cliff, mountain goats held their stately conference. The stillness was frequently broken by the canyon wren trilling a descending scale that one never forgets.

This two-thousand-acre sanctuary is called Laity Lodge. People go there for the food and to get away to something churches used to be known for, but now rarely provide — a love that means giving yourself away to others until it hurts a little and makes you light-hearted.

You have to drive up the Frio River to reach this million-dollar motel known as Laity Lodge. It is the realized vision of Howard E. Butt, Jr. of the Howard E. Butt grocery chain, known across the southwest as the H.E.B. Stores. The most fascinating people come from all over the United States to this Eden in the Texas hill country to work their way through a crisis or to rekindle the fire of their faith. Keith Miller found and left much of himself here. Now Bill Cody directs this refreshment stand, blending Texas and Madison Avenue to achieve the most effective mix of Christianity I know.

Every time I drive up that river, I have to say over and over to myself, "I don't believe in shrines." But when I get out of the car, I have to confess that my litany hasn't helped. I do believe in shrines. Burning bushes take root reliably at Laity Lodge.

I don't know whether some ground stays holy or whether a divine madness grips the participants, but the people who go to Laity Lodge keep coming back. Perhaps I can illustrate the enchantment of the place by telling how a new building originated. Mrs. Howard Butt, Sr., who is responsible for the arresting quotations chiseled in stones placed about the grounds, recently came to Laity Lodge to meet with the architect and the director. When they were all together she announced that she had just reread Bunyan's *Pilgrim's Progress* and had been entranced by the house of the wicket gate that had sheltered Pilgrim on his journey. This house was identified by a tree with two trunks growing out of the main trunk. Then Mrs. Butt suggested they drive up the canyon until they found such a tree, for she wished to build a house by the wicket gate at Laity. In a few minutes they came upon the tree, and the architect took the measurements necessary to lay out the house for the pilgrims who come to Laity.

Let me share what happened there one week in July. After breakfast, Don Williams, the young former minister to youth of Hollywood Presbyterian Church, held us rapt for an hour daily on the Book of Romans. He is both a comedian and a Ph.D from Princeton, and while we stared at the view through the window walls of the great hall and stole mint toffees from the nearby bowls, he engaged us as he has hundreds of youth in his beach ministry with the "Salt Company." After his session we leaned on the balcony outside, drinking coffee and eyeing the catfish that looked up at us from sixty feet below. We laughed and shook our heads over Don's soul-rattling suggestions. But his St. Paul had secured us too. He encouraged each of us to wear the sign: "Don't give up. God hasn't finished with me yet."

Then the bell rang and we went back into the great hall to hear psychiatrist John Knapp talk about anger. He told about the times Christ lost His temper, and about the times he lost his. Before the week was out, I felt close to this man.

John Knapp is a Christian, and he maintains there is no conflict between Scripture and psychiatry. He is humble — a humble psychiatrist who raises cattle and loves the outdoors. Instead of a couch, he and his client sit by the fireside together.

Afternoons were free for riding, hiking, and swimming in the healing river. After dinner I was supposed to say something practical about life. I can only remember one thing I said that first evening. I asked everyone if they ever remembered any time in their lives when they "had been so deliriously happy that they had rolled on the floor hugging their stomachs." I recalled my little son doing it the day I had received some good news in the mail. I suggested that there was enough good news to do it to each of us. "A time is coming for you when you'll yell: 'He died for me — O Happy Day! O Happy Day!' You'll sing it. Your feet won't keep still, and you'll quit deriding Holy Rollers."

However, the distinction of Laity Lodge is the small group of twelve to which each is assigned. Ours met outside every day on the balcony over the river, and we always took the same seats in the circle. This group was handpicked for me. I knew it the first day.

We started out to my left asking Amy to tell us how she had received her middle name. It was surprising what came out as we each answered this question. Amy was a minister's wife from Mississippi. John was a rancher. His favorite movie was *Patton,* and he had marched with the general in spirit in World War II. John was still fortyish and muscular. We took to each other immediately, and he later showed me part of his family's 38,000-acre spread which was up the road about sixty miles. Joan hastened to explain her lapful of handkerchiefs. "Please forgive me, for I always cry at these things and I can't stop. I'll be crying soon. I fear everybody thinks of me as a problem, but I've decided the only thing I can do is give my tears as an oblation to God. There I go."

Dan, a distinguished California lawyer and president of a celebrated Toastmasters Club, had first thought of making boxing a career. His reaction to being seated beside Joan was: "Not another crying woman!" Then he found himself saying something he said he'd never told anyone before: "I've always liked women, and I've never liked men." There was laughter and love enough to plunge into the question: "Do you care to share anything that has stretched you lately?" There was no pushing. Anyone could say "I pass," but many were hurting and most eager to share the load they had been carrying.

Small-group sessions can be mishandled and can make the participants suffer from overexposure. Obviously, there are some things we are only to share with God or perhaps with one other person. Paul, for instance, told the world about his "thorn in the flesh," but perhaps only Luke knew what it was. There is a time and place, and I believe that what was shared in our group was not forced but evoked. What came out was meant to come out. I was never more sure that the act of love is when one is able to share something that has been secretly hurting him — it is what we mean when we say we are loving each other. Our first two sessions were so rich and relaxed we could hardly wait to get back together Wednesday.

But a newcomer broke in Wednesday and ruined everything. He was young, handsome and proceeded to take over our group uninvited. When anyone managed to squeeze in a comment, he was on it with his wisdom. I had trouble controlling my irritation. Everything had been perfect previous to his intrusion. He shot the hour, and he promised to be back next round. A glimpse of John, the rancher, saved me. He was having a harder time than I was.

Then I noticed that everybody suddenly disappeared from the scene of the crime except Dan, who was standing in the corner of our balcony perch above the river. His back was toward me, and he was holding onto the handrails, as a boxer does in his corner between rounds. Something told me he was sobbing. I took my position beside him in silence. He was sobbing with anger and in strong language. Anger at the newcomer had ruptured his old sob story. "Dave, I never used to sit down between rounds. I couldn't wait to kill that other guy. That's why I went into the ring, and on into the courtroom." Our talkative newcomer had opened his old wound. But it didn't get inflamed. It drained.

The next day, not knowing what else to do, I suggested that perhaps the time had come for us to pray for each other. So each of us said a sentence or so to God for Amy, doing the same for each person on around the circle. I was astounded at the effect this had on all, and especially on the one prayed for — the unexpected insights, to which compassion was sensitive. When people speak to me of a prayer meeting, it makes me tired, but I cannot imagine being more royally entertained and refreshed than we were by this exchange.

Finally it was John's turn to be prayed for. He stopped us. "I've got to do something before you pray for me." Swiftly he crossed the circle in a stride and knelt before the newcomer. "Bob, you really turned me off yesterday. I hope you'll forgive me, for I want to make things right between you and me." Such an act by such a man struck us with the force of an explosion. Bob muttered an acceptance.

When it was the boxer attorney's turn to pray for Bob, he prayed: "Lord, You know how I've always hated men, and how I've wanted to put on the seven-ounce gloves with Bob since he broke in on us. I'd let him cut me a little in the first two rounds; then I'd let him have it. O God, I don't know that I can pray for him. Help me."

Our last evening together arrived, and we spent it around the table. The mood was festive — steak, celebration. "Anyone have anything to celebrate? Let's give a twenty-one-gun salute to God tonight. Fire at will."

A sculptress began with something for show and tell. She passed it around. It was a wax figurine she had been working on all week. It was of a boy rolling on the floor in laughter holding his sides. She told me she would cast it in bronze and give it to me.

A woman announced that she had always been embarrassed by her lack of skill in needlework, but a verse had occurred to her as she thought over our very special week, and she found pleasure sewing it onto a rough piece of cloth. The verse was: "And the glory of the Lord shone around *them*." Then she said: "It must be someone's birthday, and for some reason I want for us all to sing 'Happy Birthday to You.' "

With the singing of "Happy Birthday," the boxer rose to his feet to announce that it truly was his birthday in Christ. The woman gave him the pennant she had sewed, and he said: "I have something to say which requires my standing by someone." He approached my table, stopped behind me, placed his hands on my shoulders, and spoke of the anger in him that had taken him into boxing and the courtroom, and had discharged this week with the fury toward Bob. He spoke of the loneliness and desertion haunting him across the years that he had felt so acutely and desperately when he felt my presence on the balcony beside him.

A bearded young minister arose to confess that despite his vows he had never been able to tell anyone that he loved them. "My father left when I was a child, and I was forced to be father to my brother and husband to my mother. I have been hating everyone. I find that the love in this place this week has been enough to unload my bitterness, and I can say tonight, for the first time in my life, 'I love you all!' "

Then Joan stood to say: "I have arrived at the bottom of my lake. I haven't cried since yesterday. Hurrah!"

Finally a blonde starlet in dance costume stood to share the complexity of being a Christian in the entertainment world. She had asked to be last that night to praise God the way she knew: "Would you all please come with me to the great hall and make a big circle?" She stood in the center with a book from which she read. It was Psalm 150: "Praise God with the dance." While someone played the old pump organ, she flung herself into the air for God. The words to the music were these:

> I danced in the morning when the world was begun,
> And I danced in the moon and the stars and the sun.

And I came down from heaven and I danced on the
earth
At Bethlehem I had my birth.

I danced for the Scribe and the Pharisee,
But they would not dance and they wouldn't follow
me.
I danced for the fishermen, for James and John —
They came with me and the dance went on.

I danced on the Sabbath and I cured the lame;
The holy people said it was a shame.
They whipped and they stripped and they hung me
high,
And they left me there on a cross to die.

I danced on a Friday when the sky turned black.
It's hard to dance with the devil on your back.
They buried my body and they thought I'd gone —
But I am the dance and I still go on.

They cut me down and I leapt up high.
I am the life that'll never never die.
I'll live in you if you'll live in Me.
I am the Lord of the dance said He.

Dance, then, wherever you may be;
I am the Lord of the dance said He,
And I'll lead you all wherever you may be,
And I'll lead you all in the dance said He.[1]

And when the dancing was done, we all knelt in a
circle, clasping hands, and prayed to the Lord of the
dance who had once told a story about a returning prodigal son being greeted by "the sound of music and dancing."

[1]Sydney Carter, "Lord of the Dance," copyright© 1963 by Galliard Ltd. All rights reserved. Used by permission of Galaxy Music Corporation, N.Y., sole U.S. agent.

BEFORE YOU LAUGH

BEFORE
YOU
LAUGH

Jeb Magruder, of Watergate infamy, recently addressed a banquet in his new role as vice president of a national Christian youth organization. His first words were: "The only reason I am able to stand here before you this evening is because someone forgave me." The secret to laughter is not only in being timely, as with Booger's vernacular and the small-group craze, but in the rediscovery of the timeless truths. Forgiveness is the forgotten prerequisite to laughter.

Jesus' dying words were, "Forgive them," and He said them to His murderers. Those words were not said simply to make Jesus look good. They shook the earth to life. We treat Jesus' forgiving spirit as though He were only glorifying Himself. We say, "Isn't that just like Him," instead of saying, "Oh, how can I ever thank You enough." Jesus' pardon split the curtain in the temple and stampeded the mob from Calvary "beating their breasts." Jesus' forgiveness was not simply His being a good sport about what we did to Him — it was our salvation. It is the hope of the world.

Forgiveness was what men had been waiting for ever since they fell out with God. Have you heard that Good News? The curse is broken. Stop the condemnation. Start begging people's pardon. Jesus has gotten us off the hook. Pass it on. "Master, if my brother goes on wronging me how often should I forgive him? Would seven times be enough?" "No," replied Jesus, "not seven times, but seventy times seven!" (Matt. 18:21,22 PHILLIPS).

Forgiveness is what Christianity is for. Christians are ordained for this special purpose. "If you forgive anyone his sins, they are forgiven; if you do not forgive them, they are not forgiven" (John 20:23). Christians are not only authorized to forgive, we must forgive or else. "Shouldn't you have had mercy on your fellow servant just as I had on you?" (Matt. 18:33).

"And his master in anger handed him over to the jailers till he should repay the whole debt. This is how my Heavenly Father will treat you unless you each forgive your brother from your heart" (Matt. 18:34,35 PHILLIPS).

Despite forgiveness being Christianity's chief claim, Christians are the most judgmental people on earth. My own denomination is known for its pronouncements on social wrongs, not for its pardons. Churches typically call people down rather than lift them up.

Are not our preachers caricatured by their pointing fingers giving the congregation hell fire and damnation? That's no comfort. The man in the pulpit is thought of as a public prosecutor rather than as a public defender such as Christ.

Unfortunately, the congregation has become afflicted with this contagion. The preacher roasts them during the sermon; then they have roast preacher for dinner. The church service is not treated as the bread of life, but as gum to chew on. "What did you think of the new preacher?" The people of God are often known for the way they pick each other to pieces — seldom for the way they put each other back together. The judgment ministers have been meting out is now being measured back to them. As soon as several influential members become a little wearied with their prophet, they put a bug in the bishop's ear or in the ear of a district superintendent, or whatever administrator rules in that particular denomination, and by conference time or whatever he is dispatched to another charge.

I am not meaning to absolve the minister of any responsibility; I am only rediscovering that forgiveness is seldom allowed to work its magic on most of these problems. It is too quickly assumed that the only solution is to get rid of the minister. No one gave a thought to forgiving him for not studying, for not visiting his parishioners, or for going through whatever hard time he was going through. When have you heard of a minister who has been truly forgiven? It is as rare as a minister forgiving.

The judge-penitent in *The Fall* by Albert Camus strips the face off our farce of forgiveness. He confesses: "I always forgot, but I never forgave." Others of us abort forgiveness the other way around, or pervert it into an act of courtesy only, as though forgiveness were simply civil etiquette instead of an act that breaks jails. The word forgiveness has withered in our hands that have lost the meaning in the marks on His hands.

I am indebted to David DuPlessis for sharing his experience in forgiveness at the World Council on Faith and Order a few years ago. He confessed he had been a rather typical minister, reproaching people with his sermons. One day the Lord suggested to him that he stop it and start forgiving. He told the Lord, "But the people are doing things I cannot justify." The Lord answered: "Who said you had to justify them? You are to forgive them. I'll reprove the world of sin. Christ 'shall come to judge the quick and the dead.' 'Judge not that ye be not judged.' 'Quit picking the splinters out of your neighbor's eye. Remove the log from your own eye.' "

Perhaps God is saying to each minister something like this: "The trouble with your ministry is not your weak faith or lack of ability; your ministry has not yet saved the world, your message has not even gotten out of town because you haven't forgiven."

DuPlessis was thunderstruck by this realization. He left the bench and started washing feet. He stopped pointing and started embracing. "First, I forgave history. I forgave the Catholics for what they had done to the Protestants. Then I forgave the Protestants for what they had done to the Pentecostals, and finally I forgave the Pentecostals for what they had done to me." Forgiveness relieved him immediately. He was able to sleep and to wake up laughing in the Spirit. Immediately he felt at home in those churches he had previously condemned. Loving people instead of grading them, he made allowances for them as a woman will do for any child she loves. He had become public defender instead of public prosecutor.

DuPlessis told of a woman who came to a minister to be healed. She had long been ill and had never responded to medical treatment. She announced: "I have finally discovered how I may be healed. I have just read in the fifth chapter of James: 'Is any one of you sick? He should call the elders of the church to pray over him and anoint him with oil in the name of the Lord. And the prayer offered in faith will make the sick person well; the Lord will raise him up. If he has sinned, he will be forgiven.' Since you are Elder Number One in our church, I have come to you to be healed."

The minister replied: "You know that I do not believe in that kind of superstition." "Whether you do or not, I do," she said. Later the minister confessed: "I decided to humor her, for she came from a wealthy family." He agreed to come to her house, and he wrote down a little prayer on a card; however, as soon as he prayed he intended to chastise her for resorting to this naive practice of the early church. She would have to accept this inevitable illness.

He arrived at her home without oil for the anointing, but she had the oil ready and the Bible open. He gave his prayer, which closed with the words: "Lord, if it be Thy will, heal her." "David," said the minister, "I should never have said that, for as soon as I did, she was immediately healed. Finally she gently reminded me: 'Aren't you going to thank God?' " For the first time this minister spoke to a living Christ.

Think of the usual way in which such a woman might have reacted to a minister who scorned her request as that one did. She would have had no trouble collecting several others he had turned off, and they could have gone to the bishop about their unbelieving minister. Instead, she refused to judge him or even go to another minister. She loved this one. Her forgiving spirit resulted in her healing and in her minister's conversion.

A young minister in upstate New York resigned because he had lost his faith. His official board did not, however, jump condescendingly at this opportunity. They prayed and decided to keep him if they could. "But I don't believe in anything," he replied. "You believe in honesty, don't you?" "Yes." "Then preach to us about honesty, and we will pray that the rest of your faith comes back." It did — better than ever before. That board even forgave their minister for losing his faith, and I believe they all found real faith then for the first time.

There are many people who have never wronged us; we just don't like them. Often ministers excuse this by saying that we are only commanded to love others, not to like them. But I can no longer believe that. Can you believe that God loves all of us, but only likes some of us? I have come to realize that any time I dislike someone it is because I have judged him for being hypocritical or opinionated, or for being more to the left or right of where I am. But as soon as I stop judging someone and start loving him, I like him too. For to like someone is to forgive him for living, for being the way he is. Liking someone means appreciating him, understanding him, and accepting him.

In Matthew 18 Jesus says that we can make a case against a brother, and if he does not respond we can go to him with a witness; then if that fails, we can take our case before the whole church. But such a procedure usually splits a church. If one makes a case out of his grievance, people take sides. It means war. Forgiveness is the better way. It means, "I'll forget it this time, and the next, and the next. . . ."

Forgiveness of the wrong done doesn't mean approval of it. Our forgiving someone simply means that we don't occupy the judge's bench; we occupy a kneeling position on the floor washing feet.

The command to forgive does not mean we cannot be angry nor that we are not allowed to make mistakes. Some of us have not forgiven ourselves. And many of us can never forgive until we get "good and mad" first. A teen-age boy whose father had wronged him wrote Billy Graham: "Would it be all right if I punched my father in the nose, then asked him to forgive me?" I say, "Yes," if forgiveness could not come another way. Often people who are easily intimidated cannot enjoy forgiveness until they have had the pleasure of an uninterrupted verbal venting of anger first. This must usually be done with someone other than the object of their anger.

DuPlessis also brought another passage to life for

me: "Whatever you bind on earth shall be bound in heaven, and whatever you loose on earth shall be loosed in heaven" (Matt. 18:18 RSV). Did it ever occur to you that heaven cooperates in our binding and loosing of people on earth? Perhaps our church was saved from its first persecution by Stephen's loosing of Saul. One might have said that the way Stephen was stoned to death was a shame, that he wasted away a lifetime dying so young. Yet, you recall how Saul, who was holding the coats of the stone-throwers that day, had been commissioned to arrest and imprison Christians. He would have seen Stephen's death and no doubt heard only too clearly Stephen's final words as he fell: "Lord, lay not this sin to their charge." Where but from Saul did Luke learn to put into his Acts of the Apostles that Stephen's face at the last was like "the face of an angel?"

Was it not the impact of this event that knocked Saul from his horse on the way to Damascus, turning him into Paul? What else but Stephen's sacrifice of forgiveness converted the ringleader of our first persecution into the chief apostle? Isn't that what we are promised? "Whatever you loose on earth shall be loosed in heaven." I think Stephen's forgiveness worked — on Paul. If so, then that forgiveness changed the course of history. Forgiveness is not a weak way out. Any forgiving we do has the weight of heaven behind it.

Think of how Christ's forgiveness affected Peter. Peter had sworn three times that he didn't even know who Christ was. That was in Christ's crucial hour of need. After it was all over, Peter began hearing from everybody that his Master had died during the very act of forgiveness. It had swept the public off that hill beating their breasts. Now it struck Peter with cosmic force. Jesus had left word for anybody who cared to listen that He did not hold against them what they had done. That news finally broke Peter's heart. "He went out and wept bitterly," and when he came out of it he was a new man. After everything else failed, forgiveness found Peter. Not only Peter. It saved the world. "Forgive them. . . ." "Whatever you loose on earth shall be loosed in heaven." "Therefore, there is now no condemnation for those who are in Christ Jesus" (Rom. 8:1).

Perhaps it is our unforgiving stance that locks the homosexual into his predicament. As soon as he is identified, he is eliminated from our list of invitations. We are neither to condemn nor condone; we are to forgive, whether or not they appreciate it. And how many drunken, desperate convicts around us are chained to their posts because we have never let them loose by our forgiveness? "Whatsoever you loose on earth shall be loosed in heaven."

What is your attitude toward prostitutes? I knew that J. P. was a respected Presbyterian elder, but I never realized how Christian he was until his friend told me about the late night he and J. P. were strolling downtown. When a woman approached J. P. and asked if she could help him in any way, he quickly replied: "No, honey, I'm already behind at home." He was neither upholding her nor holding it against her. He was forgiving her. I wonder what happened to that girl who that night was neither used nor rejected.

I know so many fine families that are wretched because of relentless pressure never relieved by forgiveness. Many of the ten thousand junior highs who ran away from home last week left because of the unreasonable demands made upon them. They were never really forgiven for not being a boy, or for not being an athlete, or for not getting good grades. The only love they ever received was given only if they met certain conditions. Forgiveness was based on performance. Love depended on a big "IF." How many tragedies could be averted in homes right now if the father would apologize to his son instead of delivering him another sermon? All the threats and ultimatums in the world finally carry no weight at all other than to completely destroy a relationship. But how many fathers have found that the blessing of reconciliation they had prayed for was waiting for them to come down off their high horse and forgive their sons the way God had forgiven them? Or better yet, to say "I'm sorry" to sons they had wronged for years.

When we can forgive as Christ has commanded us, then people will listen to our statements about Christ. I believe this is the secret of Corrie ten Boom's powerful witness. Corrie, her beloved sister Betsie, and her father were imprisoned by the Nazis for helping Jews escape through the underground stop they ran in their Haarlem watchmaking establishment. Betsie and her father died from the mistreatment and malnutrition they suffered in the concentration camps.

After World War II Corrie was on a speaking tour in Germany:

> It was at a church service in Munich that I saw him, the former S.S. man who had stood guard at the

shower room door in the processing center at Ravensbruck. He was the first of our actual jailers that I had seen since that time. And suddenly it was all there — the roomful of mocking men, the heaps of clothing, Betsie's pain-blanched face.

He came up to me as the church was emptying, beaming and bowing. "How grateful I am for your message, Fraulein," he said. "To think that, as you say, He has washed my sins away!"

His hand was thrust out to shake mine. And I, who had preached so often to the people in Bloemendaal the need to forgive, kept my hand at my side.

Even as the angry, vengeful thoughts boiled through me, I saw the sin of them. Jesus Christ had died for this man; was I going to ask for more? Lord Jesus, I prayed, forgive me and help me to forgive him.

I tried to smile, I struggled to raise my hand. I could not. I felt nothing, not the slightest spark of warmth or charity. And so again I breathed a silent prayer. Jesus, I cannot forgive him. Give me Your forgiveness.

As I took his hand the most incredible thing happened. From my shoulder along my arm and through my hand a current seemed to pass from me to him, while into my heart sprang a love for this stranger that almost overwhelmed me.

And so I discovered that it is not on our forgiveness any more than on our goodness that the world's healing hinges, but on His. When He tells us to love our enemies, He gives, along with the command, the love itself.[1]

---

[1]Corrie ten Boom *The Hiding Place* (Old Tappan, NJ: Chosen Books, 1971), p. 215.

A TIME TO WEEP

A TIME TO WEEP

Many people have no capacity for or understanding of genuine laughter, because they have not wept. They won't cry because they think it childish or weak. How many won't cry because they think it is unchristian? They say, "How could you cry after Jesus rose from the dead and gave birth to you?" The truth is: If you cannot cry, you cannot laugh.

The most piteous people in our time are those unrepentant and obstinate unbelievers who are determined to gnash their teeth over this horrid existence. You won't catch them crying. They will wallow in despair, dry-eyed till the bitter end, or stoically endure in barely disguised bitterness. They have denounced earth as a hole dug in the darkness by a malignant deity from which not even death can deliver them. Even the light is blinding and only serves to awaken the flies. But many of these haters of life will never break down and cry. They are still and cold. Their tears have turned to ice.

The poor people in the mental hospitals cannot cry. Their illness prevents them. They are damned up by despair. They remain unmoved by heartbreak. They shriek and moan in a desert unwatered by sorrow. They sit in stony silence, staring at the wall, without the heart to cry.

It was the same with those wretched orphans crammed like animals into Hitler's concentration camps. Their eyes were sunken. Even when they were beaten the moaning was dulled, the screams were lifeless. Their tears had been frightened away.

Life can never come to such creatures until the tears come. Rage and guilt must be declared to be discharged. Tears are so vital to our welfare that Jesus included them in His Beatitudes: "Blessed are those who mourn, for they shall be comforted" (Matt. 5:4). There is no detour into joy except through Good Friday.

Friends of mine are learning this through the tragic automobile accident that has left their twenty-year-old son paralyzed from the neck down. His care costs much more than the twelve thousand dollars they pay a month. He is on a respirator constantly, and they must pound his chest frequently to help him cough up fluids. His beautiful, handmade house in the woods stands empty, his tools lying as he left them. How could one turn the volume high enough to cover such an extremity? The young man reports that Jesus has come to him in his room to help him personally. Such an enlargement would be necessary. It would take a torrent of emotion to wash one through so torturous a channel. Tears are the only transportation for a voyage such as he must make.

There was a prominent oral surgeon in Dallas. Everyone loved him, but he suffered from nagging depression and from headaches that could not be diagnosed. Perhaps his plight stemmed from neglect he suffered as a small boy while his parents were alcoholics and from the puritanical tyranny that followed at the hands of his well-meaning grandmother.

He stayed home in bed one April day while his wife was doing the washing. She heard him call her name. She hurried to the room to find him almost gone. Was it his heart? A stroke? She quickly gave him mouth-to-mouth resuscitation and heart massage without effect. Then she pulled the sheet down and found he was lying in a sea of blood. He had cut both groins. The needle with which he had given himself a local anesthetic was lying nearby. He died during the rush to the hospital. His wife was hysterical, but that is not enough. She must scream and weep loud and long in order to realize and finally accept the horror of that event. She must not prematurely adopt a pose of calm and healing.

The other night I was called to the hospital by a lovely woman, a college senior. She had been planning marriage upon graduation. During class her cheek had gone numb. A day or so later while taking notes her arm stuck in the middle of a word and would not move. After tests she was told she had multiple sclerosis. As if that were not shock enough, a nurse took the liberty of wheeling her up the hallway to show her some patients in advanced stages of that disease. She froze in horror and could not go to sleep that night. On the phone she said: "Could you please come see me tonight?" Before long she began to sob. It was not simply a ladylike cry — she was grief-stricken and shaking as the tears were torn from her.

Nothing else would do. She could not pray. She could not take a deep breath. Her throat was tight. She was stuck until her tears released her. Too many people have tried to force prayer or smiles before they allowed themselves to say "ouch."

Medical personnel often administer a hasty sedative to someone undergoing a crisis. While there are occasions when it is justified, for the most part it is far better for the person to abandon himself to his feelings than to be stupified for the moment and have to go back and live them later on. A tranquilizer does not make a person truly tranquil. That state can only come after one has been honest and open about his feelings to himself and to God, and perhaps to another person.

Is it any wonder then that women who cry so much more easily than men also outlive men?

Every single one of us needs the outlet of tears. The happiest lives must face sorrows realistically. His kingdom has not yet come on earth as it is in heaven. That is why we pray for it in the Lord's Prayer. No matter if we have "pierced the seventh veil," as Paul did, we still only see "through a glass darkly."

Jesus is certainly the "Joy of Man's Desiring," but He was also "a Man of sorrows, acquainted with grief." He wept over Lazarus and over Jerusalem. We wear His cross. Much laughter today is forced and no fun at all because it does not follow "a time to weep." We are too busy proving to ourselves that we are overjoyed. Life is not always a laugh in this vale of tears. It is also Gethsemane. At the end Jesus "cried out."

Could it be that your faith has not brought you joy because you have not yet cried out?

And finally after we have freed ourselves through our tears and are able to take the bitter with the sweet in our own lives, will we not then weep at times for someone else? "See how He loved him," they said of Jesus crying about Lazarus. Love not only knows how to rejoice — it can weep with those who weep. Dear Sister Teresa has washed the streets of Calcutta with her tears. Thank God for those who have tears to spare for someone else. Someone who believes in healing told me that those he wept for, wept over, were the ones who were healed. Is anyone weeping over New York City? Your town? Perhaps the man I've been upbraiding or praying for needs my tears instead.

Do you remember how Monica, the mother of that profligate Augustine, wept over him until he became St. Augustine? She went from priest to priest for help, while Augustine went from bad to worse. Finally she found her way to the door of the old Bishop of Madura. Seeing this woman weeping for her son, he comforted her with those unforgettable words: "My dear, it is not possible for the son of these tears to perish."

> Joy and woe are woven fine,
> A clothing for the soul divine,
> Under every grief and pine
> Runs a joy with silken twine.
> It is right it should be so;
> Man was made for joy and woe;
> And when this we rightly know,
> Through the world we safely go.

> — William Blake

THE BIBLE'S HUMOR

THE BIBLE'S HUMOR

When my great-grandfather was a little boy coming home from church in the sleigh, he shouted, "Father, see the crow!" That flip outburst on the Sabbath stopped the sleigh and saw him soundly whipped. Our fathers frowned on anything that might make light of their fearful God's Holy Book or Holy Day.

But even Dante called creation *The Divine Comedy*. And I also believe I can detect at times an air of mischief about God. Are we not made in His image? At our best, do we not then have His sense of humor? How could a somber God have made skunks, parrots, penguins, asses, men? It was not only humble of Him to be born in a barn — not simply wise to warn us He will return "like a thief in the night." Those are ways by which He introduces us to laughter.

The story of the Garden of Eden is not simply the opening scene of the greatest tragedy. It has never ceased to be a source of amusement. I don't mean the way it has been ridiculed, but rather the way it has been enjoyed. Mark Twain was not the first, nor Archie Bunker the last, to market the humor of creation. Shouldn't the God who made the garden and who made the men who tell jokes on it get some credit for the laughs?

A fall is not funny, yet did you ever see a sturdy bishop fall on the ice? That hurts, just as the fall of man, but it's funny too. Laurel and Hardy fell all over the place. That's why we fell for them. Perhaps because it is so awful to see Adam and Eve falling from Paradise, we must cry and laugh as we hear Bill Cosby explain how God had to blow the whistle on them — "Okay, everybody out of the pool!" Too much reality forces men to laugh or cry. How can anyone keep a straight face when he hears Adam telling God that eating the apple wasn't his fault: *"The woman whom thou gavest to be with me,* she gave me fruit of the tree, and I ate" (Gen. 3:12 RSV). And since Eve could not go home to mother, she explained: "The serpent beguiled me, and I ate" (Gen. 3:13 RSV).

Don't you remember the story of the frontier father who had to leave his children alone in the cabin for a few hours? He told them they could do pretty much as they pleased except for one thing. There was a can of beans on the mantel, and he warned that he didn't want anyone putting a bean up his nose. When he returned, every child had a bean up his nose. "You shall not eat of the fruit of the tree which is in the midst of the garden" (Gen. 3:3 RSV), and of course that is the only fruit we are sure Adam and Eve ate.

The story of Noah is rich with humor. Ministers have been missing it for years, but recently comedians have been featuring the possibilities in Noah's predicament. How would you feel if the person on the other end of the line said, "Noah, this is God speaking. I want you to build an ark." Out of the blue the voice comes, ordering you to build a boat in the middle of a dry spell miles from any water. And as you finally fall for it and you are up there in your driveway building this crazy thing, how are you going to explain it to the buddies you usually go bowling with? "What are you doing?" "I'm building an ark." "Why?" "God said to." "Oh!" Then imagine the developing complications of Noah's lonely pilgrimage with his embarrassed wife and the teasing the children are taking. Think of the mounting tension between Noah and the zoning board as he chases down those exotic animals and loads them and all their perfume in the midst of his suburb. Neighbors are busy on the phone talking about such a crackpot — not to God, but to the police.

Remember Abraham and Sarah? We still pray to the God of Abraham. He was the first man to make the Old Testament with God. And mixed in with the most solemn commands and promises are the most hilarious situations. God's part of the bargain was to supply a son for Abraham, but one never came. Sarah became ninety years old. Still no son. Then word came through angels that ancient Sarah would have a son. And for the first time in the Bible, the word "laugh" appears. Upon getting such a preposterous message, "Abraham fell on his face and laughed" (Gen. 17:17 RSV). Why wouldn't he laugh at the complications of maternity at ninety?

Imagine old Aunt Sadie down at the nursing home being given a careful checkup for possible malignancy because of increasing abdominal extension. And the X-rays reveal instead a perfectly live fetus. I would love to see the doctor's face. Wouldn't such an event break up a nursing home beautifully? How embarrassing!

God kept His promise to Abraham in style. Birth is always a time of laughter, but Abraham had waited so long. Sarah was so old. Isaac was both a blessing and a wink of heaven.

Joseph being sold down the Nile by his brothers was a shame, but the way Joseph graduated to a position next to Pharaoh and finally had those same brothers eating out of his hand will continue to bring down the house long after we are gone. When Goliath challenged anyone in Saul's army to fight, no one could be found except a thirteen-year-old shepherd boy named David. Goliath laughed. When God picked the political leader of the century to debate with Pharaoh, He chose a Moses who was tongue-tied. And when God decided to come to earth, He descended on a little crossroad no one had ever heard of — Bethlehem. They didn't even have sidewalks to roll up at night. That was the birthplace of David and Christ. The town Jesus grew up in was never mentioned in the Bible before. No wonder Nathaniel smirked: "Nazareth! Can anything good come from there?" (John 1:46).

I love God for loving that teen-age country girl, Mary, the way He did. It is such a laugh on pomp, on the palace and the campus, on us. What a round for the teen-agers that was. I love Joseph for believing in his dreams that Mary was pregnant by God, but thinking of Joseph and expectant Mary standing in front of the rabbi on their wedding day entertains me too. What conversations had they had? "Mary, tell me again whose baby it is." "It is God's." "Yes, of course. I knew it all the time. I dreamed it." I know that Joseph genuinely believed this beloved girl, but I also know that he was human, and I can imagine some terribly funny conversations taking place as he tried to explain Mary's condition to his Jewish mother.

Jesus makes me laugh. Is He not the source of our sense of humor? He is much more than a comedian, certainly not less. "I have come that they may have life, and have it to the full" (John 10:10). It fascinates me that John, the "disciple Jesus loved" (John 20:2), deliberately introduced Christ to the world at a rowdy wedding reception. "This, the first of his miraculous signs, Jesus performed in Cana of Galilee . . . and his disciples put their faith in him" (John 2:11). That was why His disciples believed. Surely a sober Savior would make His entrance solemnly in the usual funeral procession of threatening prophets. At least He would make His debut in no less serious undertaking than healing. But no, John insists that Jesus' first official act was extravagant — changing one hundred and twenty gallons of water into wine for a party.

Can anyone see Jesus commanding such instant fermentation unsmilingly? It was not an exceptional splurge for Him. It was characteristic of Him. This was the way He wanted to be known — the way John wanted Him known. If we had a Savior who knew how to laugh, could we come up with a more appropriate inauguration? I never heard of a wedding where anyone had that much wine. We use a cross to remind us of Him, but He suggested we remember Him by bread and wine.

Such an opening gambit as winemaking would aggravate religious types. What elder would want his Messiah kicking off his campaign behind the bar. This is laughable. It is beautiful. It is fun.

"Do not look somber as the hypocrites do" (Matt. 6:16). As Elton Trueblood interprets Jesus, "Do not look dismal." "Some people," Jesus is saying, "try to look dismal, and they have their reward. They succeed." Like the cartoonists of our time, Jesus had fun at the expense of the pompous Pharisees and scribes, the bullies and politicians of the day. Jesus never dealt with them in moderation. He had a heyday with them, to which He never subjected anyone else.

Even Jesus' withering anger against these religious superstars was edged with wit: "They are blind guides. If a blind man leads a blind man, both will fall into a pit" (Matt. 15:14). He caricatures these proud Pharisees' evangelism as a laugh: "You travel over land and sea to win a single convert, and when he becomes one, you make him twice as much a son of hell as you are" (Matt. 23:15).

He was not simply damning them. He made them look ludicrous. No one fed up with Pharisees could have heard those words without breaking up. What a devastating portrait Jesus made of those hairsplitters who were so careful about details and so careless about what mattered. He was really saying, "You Pharisees take such pains to polish the outside of the cup you drink from, never thinking to wash the inside because no one sees it. That's what kills a man" (Matt. 23:25). How could anyone have had a better laugh?

How would you have described the kind of religious life the Pharisees led? One might say it seriously: "They watch out carefully for little things and make work for themselves unnecessarily." Christ put it lightly: "They strain out gnats and swallow camels" (Matt. 23:24). The contortions the Pharisees went into for their religion amused Jesus. Can't you picture a Pharisee downing a humpy camel? I've caught myself doing the same thing — caught myself on His humor. Do you care for one or two humps? Is this how the church died — choked to death on its camels, worn out from straining gnats?

Think of the prickly personality of those Pharisaic God-men. Even though they were in uniform, sporting varsity "I'm Your God-Man" jerseys, they were dead giveaways to Christ. How could you expect one of those sourpusses to produce something sweet? "Do people pick grapes from the thorn bushes, or figs from thistles?" (Matt. 7:16). "Where the corpse is, there the vultures will gather" (Matt. 24:28 NEB). We might woodenly accuse the Pharisees of being showoffs, but Jesus laughed them off: "So when you give to the needy, do not announce it with trumpets, as the hypocrites do" (Matt. 6:2). "Don't blow your own horn."

While Jesus never laughed at anyone's expense other than the proud, His wit is evident everywhere. The disciples must have roared with merriment when Jesus named that unstable Simon "rock." Rock (Peter) was the name He gave to the man who denied three times that he ever knew Jesus. Rock was the one who fell in when he tried to walk on water. The man who "followed (Jesus) at a distance" when the going got rough was named Rock. I have known of huge men named "Tiny." The disciples must have thought that about that softy, Rocky, at first. Is it not amusing, after all Simon's unstable history, that when Jesus was asking Peter after the Crucifixion, "Do you truly love me?" Peter was surprised: "Yes, Lord, you know that I love you" (John 21:16). "Whatever led you to believe otherwise?" I think Peter was impossible, and so was John for being the only gospeller to tell this on him.

If Jesus appeared among us today, someone might praise Him as "The Prince of Peace," but He might surprise us: "Do not suppose that I have come to bring peace to the earth. I did not come to bring peace, but a sword" (Matt. 10:34). "If you don't have a sword, sell your cloak and buy one" (Luke 22:36). If someone were to introduce Him as a family man who had done so much for our homes, He might state the reverse: "I have come to turn a man against his father, a daughter against her mother, and a daughter-in-law against her mother-in-law. A man's enemies will be the members of his own household" (Matt. 10:35,36).

Finally, Jesus' parables are filled with His humor. How could you fail to win an audience with a preacher and a church musician cast as the villains in your most famous story as Jesus does in the parable of the Good Samaritan? And for a Samaritan to be the hero is a riot. The only good Samaritan was a dead one. The Samaritans were anathema to the Jews. It would be like our making a Communist or drug pusher into the hero.

One time I asked a rural midwestern elder to read the Scripture lesson for church. He began solemnly, haltingly. It was a modern version, unfamiliar to him. It was the parable of the cruel judge who didn't care for man or God (Luke 18:1-8). But a woman in need had gone to him, of all people for help. Of course, he didn't care whether she lived or died, but she was a persistent widow and kept pestering him until he couldn't stand it any more, and so he helped her in order to get rid of her, for fear she would drive him crazy. Suddenly in the midst of this unrehearsed Scripture reading to a sleepy congregation, the dignified elder burst out into uncontrollable laughter. The predicament of this judge who had at last met his match in this determined woman struck him as comical.

The parable of the man who pounded on his neighbor's door late at night to borrow food to feed his company is full of comedy, as are so many of the parables. But the parables of the lost things in Luke 15 are pertinent because they illustrate God in a good humor. The Pharisees were taunting Jesus for eating with "sinners," people who were religious rejects. Jesus answered this with three parables, the first of which was the lost sheep: "Suppose one of you has a hundred sheep and loses one of them. Does he not leave the ninety-nine in the open country and go after the lost sheep until he finds it?" (Luke 15:1-4).

The story suggests that God is a good shepherd like that, far more concerned about some nobody than about any ninety-nine, cozy, spiritual success stories. Such a God still rattles religious men. "The wisdom of God is foolishness with men." Even more surprising, when the black sheep is found the shepherd does not scold, but flings the sheep on his shoulders "rejoicing." "In the same way, I tell you, there is rejoicing in the presence of the angels of God over one sinner who repents" (Luke 15:10).

This same theme is followed in the second parable of the lost coin; and in the final parable of the lost son there is an added feature to excite the happiness of man. When the prodigal returns, his father runs to embrace him, rewarding him with a ring and an unprecedented celebration. Jesus intended that amazing father to make us think of God.

How do you picture God? How about a God running toward you, arranging a celebration for you because He is crazy about you. I think this kind of God is behind Jesus' sense of humor. When men are dying, they wonder if there will be anyone to receive them. Or if they have faith at all, they suspect their reception will create a scene as someone shows them who's boss. Did you ever think that one day you might run toward a God who would be running toward you, like the father who "fell on his son's neck and kissed him"?

PRAYER IS PLAY

PRAYER IS PLAY

Have you ever seen a baby trying to catch sunbeams? Perhaps you don't remember back that far, but playing was probably the first thing you ever did. You took a stick and it turned into a wand, or a gun, or a snake. Outside there was plenty of mud for pies, and inside there was enough paper to scissor for a month. You could build a city with a few blocks or drill an army with the fuzzies under the bed. Even little Bill Cosby, living in the inner city projects, submerged himself in the water tank above the commode and played submarine. He would flush it and cry: "Let her rise! Let her rise!" The bathroom was his sandbox, and he mastered it, finally flushing down his father's overcoat successfully.

Play is what you cannot wait to do as soon as you get home from school or work. It is fooling around for the fun of it. A professional is one who does something because he is paid. The word "amateur" means one who does something because he loves to. Play means joining the festivities until you enjoy *re-* creation. Play is the context of laughter.

You are never too old to play. I don't mean a hobby you take up with some ulterior motive such as health. Play is what you delight to do for its own sake. Dance? Shop? Doodling? Surfing? Hot rodding? What have you done since hopscotch? Colonel Sanders is said to enjoy following famous people around.

Work can become play. One man recently said about his business: "I'm like a dolphin in the ocean. I love it." My father accomplished this magic for me. He never forced me to work on the farm that we moved to in my teens. His affection for farming was so contagious it became my sandbox.

My father had Tom Sawyer's knack for enticing you into whitewashing the fence. Remember how Aunt Polly plagued Tom to death about painting that fence? Finally Tom devised a plan. When the carefree gang came by to torment poor Tom for being stuck in hard labor all day Saturday, they were shocked to see Tom savoring each stroke, so carried away by the ecstasy of whitewashing that he acted as though he didn't even know they were there. Before long everybody was begging to help. Reluctantly, Tom yielded before the pressure of high-priced keepsakes. Tom was paid aggies, toads, and fishhooks for their privilege of painting Aunt Polly's fence. Tom psyched everybody into thinking it was play.

Play can be perverted, as it was when Roman soldiers gambled beneath the cross for Christ's clothes. Playing jokes on someone at his expense is what it means to be a bad sport. Games can become gods that sap life. Play is more than playing poker, or taking a trip, or hallucinating.

Competition can overpower play. Tennis can turn into torment if you never win. All losers become poor losers after awhile, and victory is not always so sweet for the ego. Play degenerates if it becomes exclusively a matter of someone beating someone else.

Spectator sports leave something to be desired. Our professional pastimes are a beautiful part of our way of life; the tragedy comes when spectatoritis absorbs creative play. Rome fell while the sports fans were sitting there in the Colosseum drooling over spectacles. They called those shows live, but they helped kill the people. There are good books, but one can become a bookworm. There are good television shows, but one can become a tube boob.

Perhaps you saw the January 12, 1976, issue of *Time* featuring the soap operas on television. "A few years ago CBS was obliged to eliminate soap opera characters who were poor because the network was receiving piles of care packages and the endlessly frustrated romance of Alice Matthews and Steve Fram drove fans of *Another World* crazy. 'Why don't you let them get married?' wailed one viewer. 'Four times I've bought a wedding dress for the wedding — four times I've bought champagne.' '' At Princeton something like a quarter of the student body drops everything to watch ''The Young and the Restless'' each afternoon.

Television in moderation can be relaxing and entertaining. But there comes a time when we are no longer playing TV; it is playing us. How many times have I felt too rotten about the outcome of a game a thousand miles away to have time to care for someone nearby?

Nothing must rob us of real play, for all work and all artificial play not only make Jack a dull boy, but make him *deadly serious*. We cannot afford to lose the capacity to entertain ourselves unassisted. Paul Tournier claims you can predict a child's later adult happiness and success by whether he is able to entertain himself alone.

Father Christopher Mooney claims that, ''Man only plays when he is human, and is only human when he plays. . . . Civilization arises and unfolds only as play in its interpretation and proceeds to mold and shape man before it is defined as a form of cultural order. . . . Play gets rid of fixations, moralisms, self-righteousness. . . . Ritual festivity is man's highest moment. . . . Play offers freedom from pressure — freedom from everyday living. Play is living on the frontier of your imagination.''[1]

Christianity likes to play. ''Anyone who will not receive the kingdom of God like a little child will never enter it'' (Mark 10:15). Christ could have condemned us to hard labor; but it's like going fishing. ''Come, follow me, and I will make you fishers of men.'' Some religions required days walking on coals of fire and nights lying on

[1]Notes from an address delivered in Kansas City, May, 1975.

beds of spikes, but "My yoke is easy, My burden is light." Jesus said, "We piped for you, and you would not dance." Jesus was accused of being a glutton and a winebibber. They assaulted Him: "Why don't Your men fast?" He replied: "How can they fast when the Bridegroom is still with them?" He identified Himself as a bridegroom. We have already noticed how His parables were filled with feasts and comedy. The return of the prodigal still shocks the world. There was no punishment; "There was the sound of music and dancing." A bad boy came back. It set the house afire with festivity. Pharisees solemnly levied the complicated commandments necessary; it was a lot of work. Jesus had men laying down their lives eagerly to please Him.

We have long been accustomed to thinking of church as a requirement instead of a reward. We urge each other to pray and read our Bibles until, before we know it, we have twisted the blessing into a burden. It is no longer "Good News"; it has become more chores to do in an already overworked life. Instead of the relief Christ promised, church becomes our responsibility. Instead of the rock holding us up, we are holding up the rock.

Has prayer become one of your good works? Do you pray because you ought to, or because you have more fun with God than with anyone else?

Obviously prayer can be hard. Prayer can be Gethsemane. But think about prayer from God's point of view. He's your Father. You're His child. Would you like *your* child to come to you only because he knows he ought to? Would you appreciate your child writing you letters and

visiting you because he disciplined himself to do it?
When the Prodigal came home, the father didn't send him
back to school. He didn't put him to work or punish him.
He celebrated! Having his son back was like having a
party. What would please the heavenly Father more than
to have you feel that festive about going out with Him?
The Westminster Catechism says: "The chief end of man
is to glorify God and *enjoy* Him forever." When do we
start?

Creation was not hard work to God, nor was the
re-creation at Pentecost. They said it was a breeze. There
was no drudgery in the Garden. It was after Adam fell and
was forced to leave Eden that women went into labor and
men began to sweat. Christ's miracles were called works,
but they were not manufactured. They happened — like
walking on water. You cannot classify your conversion as
the culmination of your good deeds. It is by God's grace,
"That no man may boast." "It is a gift."

Perhaps the Lord does us the way Charlie Shultz does
Peanuts, or the way Michelangelo let "David" out of the
stone. *Re–creation* is like creation. It is recreation. As
Plato said: "Man is a plaything in the hands of God." He
made us to begin with, as though from mud pies. *Your*
re-creation today may seem at first like a sand castle in the
air. "Now do me, God." "If You want to You could make
me well." "Of course I want to. Be healed."

The playing is not finished when we come down to
the door of death. One would think that if God did play
with us as a cat plays with a mouse, death would be an
end to it. But no magician can compare with the Master,
particularly in the finishing touch of play with which He

surprises us. The hand that is quicker than the eye brought the multilated body of Christ back to more beautiful life. He does the last event in style. He beats every one of us at our own game. He makes it look so easy. I mean His loving us in the midst of the ugly way they worked Him over. He didn't complain about dying, "But like a lamb led before his shearers is dumb, so He opened not His mouth." It would seem He had a bitter end that He took hard, but we are also told that, "It was for the joy that was set before Him that Christ endured the Cross." Dying over the heads of those gambling Roman soldiers was Someone who knew how to play the game.

This is not unrealistic. Roy Kelley was informed two years ago that he had terminal cancer. He and his wife went home to cry — to die. Should they keep it secret? They prayed. The answer was that they should *play* about it. So they decided to put on a big party. They invited all their friends. During the festivities, Roy held up his hand to make an announcement: "You may have wondered why I called you all together. This is a cancer party. I have been told I have terminal cancer. Then my wife and I realized we are all terminal. We decided to start a new organization. It is called M.T.C. — 'Make Today Count.' You are all charter members." Since that time the organization has grown across the country. Roy has been too busy to die, pointing out the way we Christians are to play into the jaws of death — singing, loving, not losing a minute from "the joy the world cannot give nor take away."

THE LAST LAUGH

THE
LAST
LAUGH

Death is the doorway to life — not only our eventual physical death, but death now. One cannot have life without death. There are some things one has to die to in order to come alive.

I do not mean suicide. I do not mean quitting and flinging life back in God's face. But in order for us to come to birth, we must lie down and die. Gert Behanna came to this fork in her life and decided that she was like Siamese twins — one of them must die in order that the other might live. The "old man" in us has to go so that the new man can come. Haven't you ever felt yourself being pulled in opposite directions? And before we're pulled apart or before the "old man" stunts or smothers this young life in us, we have to get rid of him.

Scripture is rich with references. "I have been crucified with Christ. Therefore it is no longer I who live but Christ lives in me." Paul said: "I die every day." We need to conduct a little funeral every morning so that the new creature can stand up without so much competition from the old fellow in us. "He who would seek to save his life will lose it." The last laugh goes to the loser born anew in Christ, for he will find.

I don't think this means that we need to feel guilty for the meal we have just eaten. It doesn't mean that we won't make mistakes. And it doesn't mean we should lead lives like ascetic puritans. We worship Jesus, not John the Baptist. Jesus came that we might *live* "far more life than before." The issue is: who are you and I out for — self or God? Who am I really working for, rooting for, saving for? "Follow Me," He said. Am I? Or am I following in my own tracks?

In *Roughing It,* Mark Twain tells of being lost in Nevada in the snow until he came upon some tracks which he began to follow. Gradually he noticed more and more tracks — until he realized they were his own. He was going in circles. Whose tracks are we following? Am I trying to make a name for myself, or for Him?

C. S. Lewis often quoted a Scottish Presbyterian minister named George MacDonald, who got the gospel across in stories instead of sermons. That's the way George MacDonald converted C. S. Lewis. His *Lilith* goes like this:

Lilith was a beautiful princess who was completely overshadowed. The shadow had her under his power until it was no longer she who lived, but the shadow who lived in her. Lilith kept turning into a spotted leopardess, and she sucked the blood of anybody she could find. She used people, hooked them, lived off them. She was a vampire, a parasite.

Finally Lilith was so far gone that even when she turned back into the lovely princess, her left paw wouldn't turn back. She hid it with a glove so none of her victims would see. The fact that the paw wouldn't turn back tormented her to death. There was something wrong with that paw. It was a fist.

The forces of true love kept working on Lilith, trying to get the leopardess in her to die. Time after time she came to Adam, the father of us all, to die right, but at the last minute she would sneak off to suck blood.

Finally she agreed to die, but Adam said she had to do something first. She must unclench her left hand which was her hidden paw. "You must unclench it and let everything go you have taken that does not belong to you." But she had clenched it so long it had grown together. In despair she cried, "I can't, I can't." Then Adam said, "Then you cannot die to live." She cried, "Cut it off. Cut it off." Remember where Christ says, "If your right hand offend you, cut it off. It were better to lose a hand than to lose everything." So Adam took the sacred sword that the angel, according to legend, gave Adam after it was used to chase him from Eden, and cut it off in such a way that it would grow back her hand. At last Lilith was able to die to that self that was killing her. Even lovely

Lilith who had become the shadow's pet was saved from herself.

There was something specific Lilith had to do. She had to open that hand. You and I too must do something before we can die to this destructive self of ours. What do you have to do? Have you unclenched your hand? Take the step you are asked to take. Can you unclench it, or must it be cut off?

I'm a slow learner, but I am getting a little insight on what I have to do. I was asked to take part in an award for Elisabeth Elliot. She was introduced to the world through an inexplicable tragedy. Her young husband and his missionary colleagues were killed by a tribe of Auca Indians in Ecuador, a tribe to whom they had hoped to minister in the name of Christ.

While the world was numb from this heartbreaking massacre, Elisabeth Elliot seized it as an opportunity for the love of God. She and her little child walked into the jungle to live with these Stone Age savages who had murdered her husband and her friends.

When the history of this century is written, with its unprecedented spectaculars in space and its overwhelming wars, I do not believe they will overshadow this young widow's act of faith and courage. My seventeen-year-old son said: "Why, dad, not even John Wayne would have done that."

It was not simply an act of courtesy. She stayed until the months became years and those savages became her kinsmen. She was not the stereotype of the presumptuous missionary busily bending susceptible minds to her beliefs. She became one of them. She learned to respect them for the virtues they possessed that we only profess. The convert she made, she said, may have been herself.

That Auca jungle was not her mission field so much as a theater where the love of Christ played to save the rest of this mildly Christian world.

Do you know what was behind Elisabeth Elliot's doing that? It may be enough to help us unclench a paw.

"The only reason I was living in that strange little house in that very strange place, as a stranger, was because years before that I had prayed a prayer which Betty Scott Stamm had written another generation before me. I had copied it in my Bible when I was a teenager. The prayer said:

> Lord, I give up my own plans and purposes, all my own desires and hopes, and accept Thy will for my life. I give myself, my life, my all, utterly to Thee to be Thine forever. Fill me and seal me with Thy Holy Spirit. Use me as Thou wilt. Send me where Thou wilt. Work out Thy whole will in my life at any cost, now and forever."

Betty Scott Stamm was beheaded by Chinese Communists. Elisabeth Elliot was widowed and sent into the jungle.

I find the most striking example of losing one's life to find it in the life of Aleksandr Solzhenitsyn, the great exiled Russian author. In his *One Day in the Life of Ivan Denisovich,* which was written out of his own experiences in the wretched Stalinist concentration camps, Ivan ridicules the one Christian believer in the camp: "However much you pray, it doesn't shorten you a stitch. . . ." To which the believer replies, "For my part I am ready not merely to be bound but even to die for the name of the Lord Jesus.''[1]

Even more compelling to me than the monumental literary effort of Solzhenitsyn, which already has made him one of the most widely read authors of modern times, is this working out of the loser's blessing in his life.

During his eight years in the camps, Solzhenitsyn's parents died and his wife divorced him. Upon his release from prison he was dying of a cancer that was growing in him so rapidly that he could feel the difference in a span of twelve hours. It was at that point that he abandoned himself to God, so beautifully illustrated in three lines of the incredible prayer that came in that dark hour: "O God, how easy it is for me to believe in You. You created a path for me through despair. . . . O God, You have used me, and where You cannot use me You have appointed others." Miraculously his cancer left him as has Communist execution. And now beside our often mediocre and sometimes sick American publications in the airport newsstands, there are the numerous offerings of this prophet God raised up in the shadow of the Kremlin. Traveling abroad recently I saw his works on train seats and in bookstores, translated into the language of that country. "He who will lose his life for My sake will find it."

What are you and I to do? Most of us will not be asked to give blood. But we too are asked to die to self like this. There are not different grades of Christians. One either lives for himself or for God. But by living for God we get life back that we never had before. As Elisabeth's

[1]Aleksandr Solzhenitsyn, *One Day in the Life of Ivan Denisovich* (New York: E. P. Dutton, 1963), p. 156.

Elliot's husband, Jim, said before he laid down his life: "He is no fool to give what he cannot keep, to gain what he cannot lose."

Open your hand.

GOD WILL WIPE AWAY EVERY TEAR

Before we finish with laughter, let's hear from that profound theologian, Erma Bombeck.

In church the other Sunday I was intent on a small child who was turning around smiling at everyone. He wasn't gurgling, spitting, humming, kicking, tearing the hymnals, or rummaging through his mother's handbag. He was just smiling. Finally, his mother jerked him about and in a stage whisper that could be heard in a little theater off Broadway said, "Stop that grinning! You're in church!" With that, she gave him a belt and as the tears rolled down his cheeks added, "That's better," and returned to her prayers.

We sing, "Make a joyful noise unto the Lord" while our faces reflect the sadness of one who has just buried a rich aunt who left everything to her pregnant hamster. We chant, "If I have not charity, I am become a sounding brass or a tinkling cymbal." Translated in the parking lot it comes out, "And the same to you, fella!"

Suddenly I was angry. It occurred to me the entire world is in tears, and if you're not, then you'd better get with it. I wanted to grab this child with the tear-stained face close to me and tell him about my God. The happy God. The smiling God. The God who had to have a sense of humor to have created the likes of us. I wanted to tell him He is an understanding God. One who understands little children who pick their noses in church because they are bored. He understands the man in the parking lot who reads the comics while his wife is attending church. He even understands my shallow prayers that implore, "If you can't make me thin, then make my friends look fat." I wanted to tell him I've taken a few lumps in my time for daring to smile at religion. By tradition, one wears faith with the solemnity of a mourner, the gravity of a mask of tragedy, and the dedication of a Rotary badge.

What a fool, I thought. Here was a woman sitting next to the only light left in our civilization — the only hope, our only miracle — our only promise of infinity. If he couldn't smile in church, where was there left to go?[1]

Where does the smile of a child come from? I mean the wide one — the smile that is contagious — that comes from the heart and spreads from ear to ear; the kind of smile your friends have on their faces when they are about to spring a surprise birthday party on you. That is

[1] Erma Bombeck, *At Wit's End,* Publishers—Hall Syndicate.

where Christianity began, with a smile like that. Jesus is where the joy is. Tragically the church has often done what the mother did to her child. We have come to think of Jesus as coming to spank us. Oh, no! He is throwing this party for you!

Of course, the child's smile is from love, out of being loved; but if it's love, it is forever. If love is limited, it is not love. If a father tells his child, "I'll love you deeply, son, till you're twelve, and that's it" — that's not love. If we say, "For God so loved the world for the time being, or for your lifetime only, or only in case of rain, or providing you are careful"; or if it were promised that God will love you if you are good, or until you grow senile, then it isn't love at all. It is not love if it is conditional or if it is good only during a bargain sale offer. If love has an expiration date marked on it, it isn't love; it's a fad or a temporary distraction. If God says He loves you, then you can count on it after the sun stops coming up. No coronary can interfere. Love is something the bottom will not drop out of. Love cannot be interrupted. The symbol for hope is an anchor, and hope is anchored in love. Unless love is eternal, it is puppy love.

Joy is where Jesus is, and Jesus is also where the future is. This is not pie in the sky to distract us from our work here. Such joy helps us concentrate on the job to be done now. Those who are most sure of heaven do their best on earth.

A football player played for the great Lou Little. He was a high school all-American, but never played up to his potential in college. In his senior year he received news that his father was dying.

The young man went to Coach Little and asked permission to miss practice in order to go home and be with his father during his last hours. The coach agreed and told the player not to worry about getting back for the game on Saturday. In three years of varsity competition he had been used only sparingly, not playing enough to qualify for a letter.

On Friday Coach Little received a telegram from the young man stating that his father had passed away and that he would be returning immediately to be with the team at the game on Saturday. The team had not won a game in two starts, and they were entering the game on Saturday as the decided underdog.

To say the least the coach was surprised when the young man knocked on his door and asked to see him prior to the game. Coach Little welcomed him and expressed his condolences, reiterating that it was not necessary for him to have hurried back. (Since he probably would not get to play anyway.) The young man said, "Coach, I want to play. Give me a chance to start!" Coach Little, a compassionate person, finally said, "Okay, I'll put you in the starting line-up."

The other team won the toss and elected to receive. Several eyebrows were raised when Coach Little announced that the young man would be in the starting line-up.

On the kickoff he was the first man down the field and made a solid tackle. Coach Little was so impressed that he allowed the young man to remain on the field with the defensive team at a linebacking position — a position he never played, since he was primarily an offensive player. He made the next three tackles. On the fourth down, Coach Little sent word in for him to play safety and receive the punt.

He gathered the ball in on his own forty-yard line and streaked down the sideline untouched into the end zone for the first score of the game. The final score was thirty-five to zero. He scored five touchdowns, made fifteen individual tackles, and had several assists. His outstanding play gained him "Player of the Week" recognition by the sportswriters.

He continued the same style of play throughout the remainder of the season and was named to the all-American team.

After the season was completed, Coach Little called the young man into his office for a conference. "What turned you around? Did your father say something to you before he died?"

The young man replied: "No, my father was dead when I arrived home. You see, my father and I were very close; we loved one another very much. At the time I entered high school, he became blind and our relationship grew even stronger. He never did get to see me play football. That Saturday — the time I returned from his funeral — was the first time he saw me play."[2]

The next world is watching the game. We are playing for keeps. There are proofs of this eternal life in the lives of those around us now.

Charles Allen tells of a boy who lost his father and mother when he was eleven years old. He was told that his aunt would take him into her home. Late one night

[2]This story was told to me by William Abare, Vice-President of Flagler College, St. Augustine, Florida.

someone came to take him to his aunt. It was a long drive.

"Will she be there?"

"Oh, yes, she'll be waiting up for you."

"Will I like living with her?"

"My son, you have fallen into good hands."

"Will she love me?"

"She has a big heart."

"Will I have my own room?"

"Yes, she has already made arrangements for you."

"Will she let me keep a puppy?"

"I think she already has some surprises for you."

It must have been two o'clock when they arrived. The light was still on, and his aunt was waiting on the porch. She hugged him to her and took him into her home. That was where he grew up. It was always a place of enchantment for him because of her. It awed him that such a replacement existed — that there was a place for him, someone waiting up for him. He had left a house of death, and she had given him a second home.

Years later, long after he had moved away, she wrote in a quavering hand to tell him that death was near and her faith was falling low about what was to become of her. He wrote to her about her future.

> Years ago when I was a boy, I left a house of death, not knowing where I was to go, whether anyone cared, whether it was the end of me. The drive was long and the driver encouraged me. Finally, he pointed out your light to me. Then we were in the yard, and there you were — embracing me and taking me by the hand to the room that you had made up. After all these years I can't believe it — how you did all this for me. I was expected. I felt so safe in that room — so welcome. It was my room.

Now it's your turn to go, and as one who has tried it out, I'm writing to let you know someone's waiting up for you. Your room is all ready. The light will be on. The door will open as you drive into the yard. Don't worry, Auntie, you are expected. I know for sure, for I once saw God standing in your doorway long ago.

I saw God coming back for us in something that touched my heart long ago. I remember going home from the Navy for the first time during World War II. Home was so far out in the country that when we went hunting, we had to go toward town. We had moved there for my father's health when I was thirteen. We raised cattle and horses. Some who are born on a farm regard the work and the solitude as a chore, but coming from town, as I did then, made that farm home an Eden to me.

We lived in a beautiful bank house that had been built from bricks made on the place by the first settlers in the northwest territory. (A bank house was one where you could step into the second story from ground level on one side or step into the first story on the lower side.) There was no heat upstairs at all, and I slept in a room with the window-door open all winter in sub-zero weather. I was under about ten blankets and often under a blanket of snow. I got up at five o'clock in the dark and ate breakfasts of sausage we butchered and seasoned in our own smokehouse.

I realize some of us can look back on our youth and glamorize a life that we actually disliked at the time; but I can honestly say that to me the world of my youth in that isolated wilderness was a place of enchantment. I remember boarding the school bus and smelling skunk coming from some boy whose traps had missed the muskrat. I remember the fever of work at threshing time and those threshing dinners. Women outdoing each other killing men with pie.

I was entranced when we drove up the mile-long lane to see the old place for the first time — a beautiful example of decaying splendor. The back screen door had a hole in it. When we went inside, there was a pet pig asleep by the fire.

The descendants of the original settlers were still there. They were two maiden ladies who had been teachers till they lost their hearing. One used a hearing trumpet. Her name was Maggie, and she had a heart of gold. Maggie went with the place. She stayed on with my father and mother, sister and me after we bought the farm. I met her sister, Sarabelle, as I came around the house to the backyard for the first time. It was August, and Sara was making peach butter in a huge black kettle that she stirred with a long wooden hoe to keep her away from the fire.

I started a little flock of Shropshire sheep, the kind that are completely covered by wool except for a black nose and the tips of black legs. My father helped them have their twins at lambing time, and I could tell each one of the flock apart at a distance with no trouble. I had a beautiful ram. A poor man next door had a beautiful dog and a small flock of sheep he wanted to improve with my ram. He asked me if he could borrow the ram; in return he would let me have the choice of the litter from his prize dog.

That is how I got Teddy, a big, black Scottish shepherd. Teddy was my dog, and he would do anything for me. He waited for me to come home from school. He slept beside me, and when I whistled he ran to me even if he were eating. At night no one would get within a half mile without Teddy's permission. During those long summers in the fields I would only see the family at night, but Teddy was with me all the time. And so when I went away to war, I did not know how to leave him. How do you explain to someone who loves you that you are leaving him and will not be chasing woodchucks with him tomorrow like always?

So, coming home that first time from the Navy was something I can scarcely describe. The last bus stop was fourteen miles from the farm. I got off there that night about eleven o'clock and walked the rest of the way home. It was two or three in the morning before I was within a half mile of the house. It was pitch dark, but I knew every step of the way. Suddenly Teddy heard me and began his warning barking. Then I whistled only once. The barking stopped. There was a yelp of recognition, and I knew that a big black form was hurtling toward me in the darkness. Almost immediately he was there in my arms. To this day, that is the best way I can explain what I mean by coming home.

What comes home to me now is the eloquence with which that unforgettable memory speaks to me of God. If my dog, without any explanation, would love me and take me back after all that time, would not my God?

Jesus saw this far more memorably as He described that old father running to meet his long-lost, returning son. "If you then, who are evil, know how to give good gifts to your children, how much more will your Father

who is in heaven give good things to those who ask him!"
(Matt. 7:11 RSV).

My dear friends, they are never weary of telling us
that life is no laughing matter. But it all depends upon the
way earth is punctuated. The point is that one day all will
be well. Knowing this takes the sting out of the mean time.
The returning prodigal was absolutely bewildered, as our
age is, by his father's reckless forgiveness and extravagant
love. When he was so utterly lost and alone, he was
found. At the end of his rope, at last he came into an
incredible kingdom. The fattest calf, the warmest coat,
and the costliest ring were his. "There was the sound of
music and dancing." I tell you — Jesus makes me laugh.

There is no other blessing I can give you, no gift so
precious, no treasure so refreshing, nothing that can pro-
vision you for the journey we are all making, than to tell
you that Someone is searching diligently for you. He is
not a stationary God. He is crazy about you. The expense
to which He has gone isn't reasonable, is it? The Cross
was not a very dignified ransom. To say the least, it was a
splurge of love and glory lavishly spent on you and me:
"While we were yet sinners, Christ died for the ungodly."
"A shepherd having a hundred sheep, if he loses one,
leaves the ninety-nine to go after the one and searches
diligently until he finds it."

God is like that shepherd. That is enough to make me
laugh and cry.